Toronto
Maple Leafs

Erin Butler

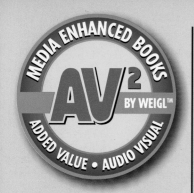

AV² provides enriched content that supplements and complements this book. Weigl's AV² books strive to create inspired learning and engage young minds in a total learning experience.

Your AV² Media Enhanced books come alive with...

Audio
Listen to sections of the book read aloud.

Key Words
Study vocabulary, and complete a matching word activity.

Go to www.av2books.com, and enter this book's unique code.

Video
Watch informative video clips.

Quizzes
Test your knowledge.

BOOK CODE

T 8 7 5 5 2 3

Embedded Weblinks
Gain additional information for research.

Slide Show
View images and captions, and prepare a presentation.

AV² by Weigl brings you media enhanced books that support active learning.

Try This!
Complete activities and hands-on experiments.

... and much, much more!

Published by AV² by Weigl
350 5th Avenue, 59th Floor
New York, NY 10118
Websites: www.av2books.com   www.weigl.com

Library of Congress Control Number: 2014951947

ISBN 978-1-4896-3188-6 (hardcover)
ISBN 978-1-4896-4018-5 (softcover)
ISBN 978-1-4896-3189-3 (single-user eBook)
ISBN 978-1-4896-3190-9 (multi-user eBook)

Printed in the United States of America in Brainerd, Minnesota
1 2 3 4 5 6 7 8 9 0 19 18 17 16 15

032015
WEP050315

Senior Editor Heather Kissock
Art Director Terry Paulhus

Photo Credits
Every reasonable effort has been made to trace ownership and to obtain permission to reprint copyright material. The publishers would be pleased to have any errors or omissions brought to their attention so that they may be corrected in subsequent printings.

Weigl acknowledges Getty Images and iStock as its primary image suppliers for this title.

Toronto Maple Leafs

CONTENTS

Introduction

As one of the **Original Six** National Hockey League (NHL) teams, the Toronto Maple Leafs have had a long and storied history. When the NHL began play in 1917, Toronto was awarded a team. The **franchise** enjoyed a successful start, winning two Stanley Cups in its first five NHL seasons. Before the NHL **expanded** in 1967, the Maple Leafs and Montreal Canadiens were the league's two most dominant teams.

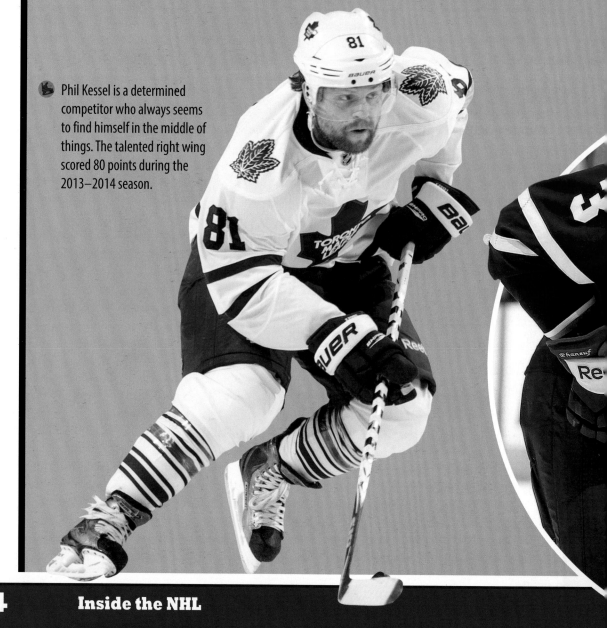

Phil Kessel is a determined competitor who always seems to find himself in the middle of things. The talented right wing scored 80 points during the 2013–2014 season.

The Leafs, however, have not won a Stanley Cup since. They suffered through losing seasons from 2005 through 2012, but in 2013, the team finally broke through, punching their ticket into the **playoffs** with 57 points. Fans in Toronto have plenty to cheer about as Phil Kessel, James van Riemsdyk, Dion Phaneuf, and several other young and talented players chase more Stanley Cup glory.

Star defenseman Dion Phaneuf was traded from the Calgary Flames to Toronto during the 2009–2010 season.

Toronto
MAPLE LEAFS

Arena Air Canada Centre

Division Atlantic

Head Coach Peter Horachek

Location Toronto, Ontario, Canada

NHL Stanley Cup Titles 1918, 1922, 1932, 1942, 1945, 1947, 1948, 1949, 1951, 1962, 1963, 1964, 1967

Nicknames Leafs

65
Playoff appearances

2
Retired numbers

13
Stanley Cup titles

70
Hall of Famers

History

The Maple Leafs have made the Stanley Cup Final **TWENTY-ONE** times, bringing home the Cup in all but eight appearances.

Posing for photos along with the Stanley Cup was a regular occurrence for Conn Smythe and the Leafs during the 1940s.

When the Toronto franchise began play in the NHL in 1917, they were first known as the Arenas. They later became known as the St. Patricks or St. Pats, to appeal to Toronto's large Irish population. They changed names to the Maple Leafs after Conn Smythe bought the team and quickly became a national symbol for Canadian hockey. Local support for the team grew during this time period as well, particularly after broadcaster Foster Hewitt began calling games on the radio. This brand new idea of Smythe's furthered the Leafs' following and changed the NHL.

Smythe's tactics on the ice brought the Maple Leafs great success as well. The team won 13 Stanley Cups from 1918 to 1967, second only to the Canadiens, who won 14 during that time period. In the 1940s, behind the play of legends such as Ted Kennedy and Syl Apps, the Leafs captured five Cups. Roster changes limited the Leafs during the 1950s, but they returned to glory under head coach Punch Imlach in the 1960s. The winning, however, stopped after 1967, the last time the Leafs won the Cup.

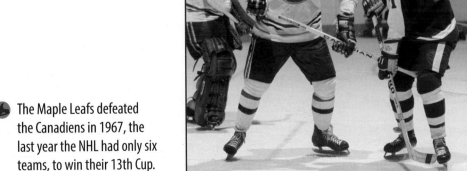

The Maple Leafs defeated the Canadiens in 1967, the last year the NHL had only six teams, to win their 13th Cup.

The Arena

The Air Canada Centre replaced the beloved Maple Leaf Gardens.

The Maple Leafs have played in a number of arenas. They began play at the Mutual Street Arena in 1917, followed by a long run at Maple Leaf Gardens from 1931 until 1999. They finally settled at the larger Air Canada Centre in 1999 and have remained there to this day. Maple Leaf Gardens was well loved by fans for nearly 70 seasons, but with 18,200 seats, luxury suites, and greatly improved technology, the Air Canada Centre was a major upgrade.

The new arena has been filled to capacity for nearly every home game the Leafs have played. In addition to hosting Maple Leafs home games, the arena also hosts the Toronto Raptors of the National Basketball Association (NBA) and Toronto Rock of the National Lacrosse League (NLL). Besides sporting events, the arena also hosts concerts, ice shows, and conventions.

The Air Canada Centre is an important part of downtown Toronto and is now a familiar feature of the city's skyline. The inside of the arena is well known for its accessible seating, beautiful walkways, and historical Maple Leafs artifacts.

The Maple Leafs share their arena with the Raptors, who play 41 regular season home games per season at the Air Canada Centre.

Where They Play

British Columbia **7**

Alberta **4**

3

CANADA

Saskatchewan

Manitoba **14**

Ontario

Washington

Montana

North Dakota

Minnesota **11**

Wisconsin **8**

Oregon

Idaho

South Dakota

UNITED

Iowa

Illinoi

Nevada **6**

Wyoming

Nebraska

STATES

Utah

Colorado **9**

Kansas

Missouri **13**

California

Arizona **2**

5

1

New Mexico

Oklahoma

Arkansas

Pacific Ocean

Texas **10**

Louisiana

MEXICO

Gulf of Mexico

PACIFIC DIVISION

1 Anaheim Ducks
2 Arizona Coyotes
3 Calgary Flames
4 Edmonton Oilers

5 Los Angeles Kings
6 San Jose Sharks
7 Vancouver Canucks

CENTRAL DIVISION

8 Chicago Blackhawks
9 Colorado Avalanche
10 Dallas Stars
11 Minnesota Wild

12 Nashville Predators
13 St. Louis Blues
14 Winnipeg Jets

Newfoundland

Quebec

Prince Edward Island

New Brunswick

New Hampshire

Vermont

Maine

Nova Scotia

20

Air Canada Centre, Toronto

22

19

15

Massachusetts

26

Rhode Island

27

New York

25

Connecticut

17

16

New Jersey

Michigan

Pennsylvania

29

Ohio

28

Delaware

Maryland

30

Indiana

24

West Virginia

Virginia

District of Columbia

Kentucky

23

North Carolina

Tennessee

12

South Carolina

Alabama

Georgia

Atlantic Ocean

pi

Florida

21

18

Air Canada Centre

AIR CANADA CENTRE

Arena
Air Canada Centre

Location
40 Bay Street
Toronto, ON M5J 2X2

Broke Ground
March 12, 1997

Completed
February 19, 1999

Features
- creative design for good sightlines
- 12-story Air Canada Tower
- galleria walkway

LEGEND
☆ Air Canada Centre
▪ Eastern Conference
▪ Western Conference

NHL EASTERN CONFERENCE

ATLANTIC DIVISION		METROPOLITAN DIVISION	
15 Boston Bruins	19 Montreal Canadiens	23 Carolina Hurricanes	27 New York Rangers
16 Buffalo Sabres	20 Ottawa Senators	24 Columbus Blue Jackets	28 Philadelphia Flyers
17 Detroit Red Wings	21 Tampa Bay Lightning	25 New Jersey Devils	29 Pittsburgh Penguins
18 Florida Panthers	☆ 22 Toronto Maple Leafs	26 New York Islanders	30 Washington Capitals

The Uniforms

The Maple Leafs began putting player names on jerseys in 1977.

The maple leaf design first appeared on the uniforms in 1927, but the colors remained green and white until the 1928 season.

When the Toronto franchise started out as the Arenas, the team had a very simple blue uniform featuring the letter "T" for Toronto. When the Arenas became the St. Pats a few years later, they changed their colors to green and white. A year after they were renamed the Maple Leafs, they changed their colors back to blue and white. Since that time, the uniforms have undergone only minor changes. The maple leaf has remained the team's crest, although it has also changed slightly over the years.

On the front of today's uniform is the team crest, a maple leaf with the words "Toronto Maple Leafs" printed on it. The blue jersey for home games has a white leaf, while the away jersey is white and has a blue leaf. Both uniforms feature a more detailed leaf as shoulder patch.

HOME

AWAY

Toronto's locker room pays tribute to the maple leaf, which is a key part of the Maple Leafs' identity, in addition to being the national symbol of Canada.

Helmets and Face Masks

Maple Leafs player numbers appear at the top center of the new Reebok Edge helmet, introduced in **2007**.

The maple leaf design was added to the team's helmet in 1997.

Toronto's **logo** is a maple leaf with 11 points on it, and the words "Toronto Maple Leafs" in the center. For home games, the Leafs wear a blue helmet with a white leaf and blue lettering. For away games, the colors are reversed.

Unlike position players, goalies are able to create unique designs on their helmets. This has become an NHL tradition and is a source of pride for goaltenders. In Toronto, Leafs goaltenders have used their helmets as both a place to pay respects to the franchise's deep roots, and also as an opportunity to have some fun. Andrew Raycroft's mask featured portraits of famous players in Maple Leaf history, while Vesa Toskala went for a different look, with a monster on his mask. Curtis Joseph's mask was perhaps the most fearsome of all, showing a beast with large fangs designed to look like they were part of the goaltender's face.

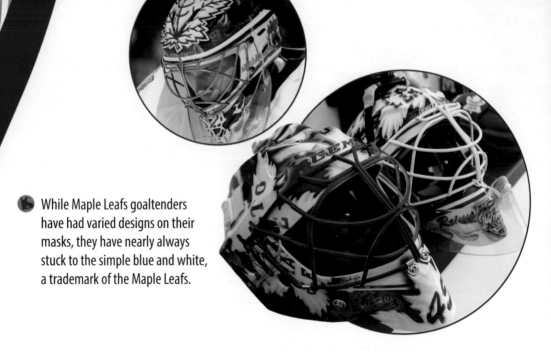

While Maple Leafs goaltenders have had varied designs on their masks, they have nearly always stuck to the simple blue and white, a trademark of the Maple Leafs.

The Coaches

41 The Maple Leafs have had 41 head coaches since their founding.

Current Interim coach Peter Horachek has a particularly tough job, coaching one of the most successful franchises in NHL history. The expectations are high, and anything short of the Cup is deemed a failure.

The Maple Leafs have gone through a number of coaches in their long history. One trait that the best coaches share is creativity, and that is certainly true for many of the Leafs' leaders. Many imaginative Maple Leafs coaches have built lineups that best deploy the unique skills of their players. A few still hold a special place in franchise history.

HAP DAY A former captain for the Maple Leafs, Hap Day was a cheerful coach who led the Leafs to their incredible success in the 1940s. He knew the NHL rules inside and out, and was very demanding of his players. As head coach for the Leafs, he won five Stanley Cup titles. He was inducted into the Hall of Fame in 1961.

PUNCH IMLACH Punch Imlach is perhaps the best example of creativity in Toronto coaching. While he valued loyalty and veteran players, he was also imaginative and had the idea to turn Red Kelly from a defenseman into a center. He has also been inducted into the Hall of Fame.

PETER HORACHEK After one season as the head coach of the Florida Panthers, Peter Horachek took an assistant coaching role with the Maple Leafs in 2014. Horachek settled in and worked for the Leafs' head man, Randy Carlyle. Despite posting a winning record, Carlyle left 40 games into the 2014–2015 season. In his place, Horachek assumed leadership of the Maple Leafs with a playoff berth in sight.

Fans and the Internet

Maple Leafs fans brave the chilly winter weather to support their team during rare outdoor games.

The tradition of dedicated Maple Leafs fans dates back to Foster Hewitt's radio broadcasts in the 1920s. At the time, before TV even existed, the Leafs were the first NHL team to broadcast their games on the radio. This new way of following hockey captured the hearts of Canadian fans and laid the foundation for one of the greatest fan bases in all of professional sports. Maple Leafs fans are now known proudly as Leafs Nation. Today, despite nearly a half century without a Cup, the arena seats fill up nightly, and fans throughout Toronto and greater Canada tune in on their TVs to catch a glimpse of their Leafs.

Not surprisingly, Leafs fans are very active online. They visit blogs and news websites such as The Leafs Nation and Maple Leafs Hot Stove, as well as the official Leafs message board. The franchise is also active in social media, connecting fans using Twitter and Facebook.

Signs
of a fan

#1 Fans are fond of the team's **mascot**, Carlton the Bear, who goes to games wearing a Maple Leafs jersey.

#2 Maple Leafs tickets are among the most expensive in the NHL, yet fans still line up for the chance to attend a home game at the Air Canada Centre.

Legends of the Past

Many great players have suited up for the Leafs. A few of them have become icons of the team and the city it represents.

Dave Keon

Dave Keon was an offensive powerhouse, in addition to being a tough-as-nails defensive player for the legendary Maple Leafs team of the 1960s. The speedy center was a true two-way player, and was also well known for being a class act both on and off the ice. In fact, Keon was awarded the Lady Byng Memorial Trophy, as the player who exhibited the best sportsmanship, twice. His play on the ice was equally impressive. Keon won the Calder Memorial Trophy for **rookie** of the year, and also won the Conn Smythe Trophy as the Most Valuable Player (MVP) during the 1967 Stanley Cup playoffs.

Position: Center
NHL Seasons: 18 (1960–1975, 1979–1982)
Born: March 22, 1940, in Rouyn-Noranda, Quebec, Canada

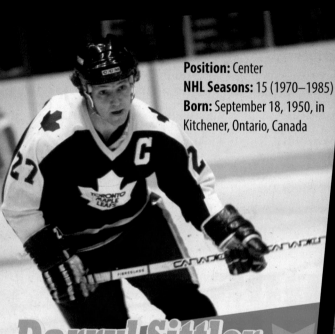

Position: Center
NHL Seasons: 15 (1970–1985)
Born: September 18, 1950, in Kitchener, Ontario, Canada

Darryl Sittler

Captain and center Darryl Sittler was a bright spot for the Maple Leafs in an otherwise bleak decade of the 1970s. Although he never won a championship with the Leafs, Sittler was a star offensive player who racked up points. In a record-setting game in 1976, he recorded an astonishing 10 points, including two separate **hat tricks**. He logged an impressive total of 20 career hat tricks. Despite often feuding with Leafs' management, Sittler is remembered fondly in Toronto. He was inducted into the Hall of Fame in 1989.

Frank Mahovlich

Known as "The Big M," Frank Mahovlich was a key offensive player for the Maple Leafs during the successful 1960s seasons in Toronto. The left wing had a big **slap shot** and was not afraid to lay a hit on an opponent. He won the Calder Memorial Trophy as a rookie, but felt great pressure to succeed from both fans and coaches alike, which ultimately affected his play negatively. Later, he was traded to the Detroit Red Wings and then to the Canadiens, where his game improved. Mahovlich was elected into the Hall of Fame in 1981.

Position: Left Wing
NHL Seasons: 18 (1956–1974)
Born: January 10, 1938, in Timmins, Ontario, Canada

Borje Salming

Swedish-born Borje Salming paved the way for European players in the NHL, and Swedish players in particular. A scout for the Maple Leafs sought him out after seeing him play in Europe, and Salming joined the team. In addition to his stamina and his puck-handling skills, he had the important combination of being a defenseman with superior offensive skills. When he was inducted into the Hall of Fame in 1996, he became the first Swede to receive such an honor.

Position: Defenseman
NHL Seasons: 17 (1973–1990)
Born: April 17, 1951, in Kiruna, Sweden

Stars of Today

Today's Leafs team is made up of many young, talented players who have proven that they are among the best in the league.

Phil Kessel

Phil Kessel began his NHL career with the Boston Bruins and was traded to the Maple Leafs in 2009. Kessel is an explosive scorer and a highly skilled skater. What is perhaps most impressive about Kessel is his determination. During his rookie season, he was diagnosed with cancer, but he recovered and continued playing. For his heroic efforts, Kessel was given the Bill Masterton Memorial Trophy in 2007, an award for dedication. Since his recovery, he has been an inspiration to his team, and his community, going to great lengths to raise awareness about cancer.

Position: Right Wing
NHL Seasons: 9 (2006–Present)
Born: October 2, 1987, in Madison, Wisconsin, United States

Dion Phaneuf

As the current captain for the Maple Leafs, Dion Phaneuf is a talented leader. Phaneuf started his NHL career with the rival Calgary Flames, but has since become the heart and soul of the Maple Leafs. Although Phaneuf is a defenseman, he is known for having great offensive timing, always seeming to attack at the key moment of the game. His size and strength make him nearly immovable, helping him to become widely recognized within the league. Phaneuf has played in three NHL **All-Star** games.

Position: Defenseman
NHL Seasons: 10 (2005–Present)
Born: April 10, 1985, in Edmonton, Alberta, Canada

James van Riemsdyk

James van Riemsdyk is a fairly new addition to the Maple Leafs, joining the team in June 2012. Van Riemsdyk is a young, talented player who seems to be shaking off his developmental years while fast becoming a true NHL talent. Although he is not yet a top scorer in the league, van Riemsdyk is an accurate shooter with superior ice speed. With his skills and large stature, he has all the makings of a great player. As he continues to grow with the Leafs, van Riemsdyk's playing future looks bright.

Position: Left Wing
NHL Seasons: 5 (2009–Present)
Born: May 4, 1989, in Middletown, New Jersey, United States

Joffrey Lupul

Joffrey Lupul is a seasoned NHL veteran who joined the Maple Leafs in February 2011. The left wing is big enough to handle himself against NHL defensemen and has good hands and a great shot as well. Lupul wears his number, 19, as a tribute to his heroes, hockey legends Joe Sakic and Steve Yzerman. Although he is not among the league's leaders in any one category, his great creativity around the opposition's net makes him difficult to guard. Lupul has recorded three career hat tricks and played in the 2012 All-Star Game.

Position: Left Wing
NHL Seasons: 10 (2003–Present)
Born: September 23, 1983, in Fort Saskatchewan, Alberta, Canada

All-Time Records

302
Wins as Goaltender
Turk Broda played his entire NHL career for the Maple Leafs and racked up the most wins in net for the Leafs.

420
Goals
Although he never won a championship with the Maple Leafs, Mats Sundin was an explosive scorer, and his goal record is yet to be broken.

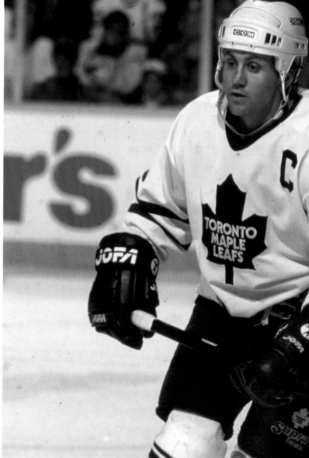

1,187
Games Played
From 1949 to 1971, George Armstrong played for the Maple Leafs. During that time, he set a team record for games played.

1.14
Most Assists Per Game
Doug Gilmour was a talented Maple Leaf during the rebuilding years of the 1990s. He set a team record for average **assists** per game during the 1992–1993 season.

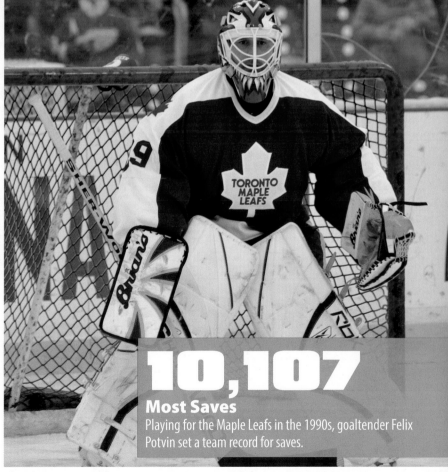

10,107
Most Saves
Playing for the Maple Leafs in the 1990s, goaltender Felix Potvin set a team record for saves.

Timeline

Throughout the team's history, the Maple Leafs have had many memorable events that have become defining moments for the team and its fans.

1917
On November 26, the NHL is founded. Toronto receives a franchise, which is first known as the Arenas, then as the St. Pats, and finally as the Maple Leafs. They play their first game on December 19, 1917.

1931
Conn Smythe signs defensive great, King Clancy. The same year, Smythe gets the idea to have Foster Hewitt broadcast Leafs games on the radio.

1912   1916   1920   1924   1928   1932

The Toronto Arenas win their first Stanley Cup in franchise history against the Vancouver Millionaires in five games.

1942
The Maple Leafs begin their dominance of the 1940s with a Stanley Cup championship win over the Detroit Red Wings.

The Future

It is undeniable that the Maple Leafs of today are not the league giants that played in the 1940s and 1960s. The NHL expansion of 1967 made winning the Stanley Cup harder for every team. However, with a healthy mix of skilled young players and experienced veterans, along with a commitment to creative coaching, the Leafs have a promising future.

1967

With a victory over the Canadiens in Game 6, the Leafs win their last Stanley Cup, the 13th in their history.

Darryl Sittler plays an incredible game against the Boston Bruins in which he records six goals and four assists for a record-breaking total of 10 points.

1970 · **1980** · **1990** · **2000** · **2010** · **2020**

1999

On February 13, the Maple Leafs play their last game at the famous Maple Leaf Gardens, a loss to the Chicago Blackhawks. The team would later move to the Air Canada Centre.

2013

After missing the playoffs for seven straight seasons, the Maple Leafs finally reach the postseason again in 2012–2013. Their stay is short, though, as the Bruins eliminate them in the first round.

2000

By defeating the Tampa Bay Lightning on April 8, the Maple Leafs finish the season with 100 points for the first time in their history.

Write a Biography

Life Story

A person's life story can be the subject of a book. This kind of book is called a biography. Biographies often describe the lives of people who have achieved great success. These people may be alive today, or they may have lived many years ago. Reading a biography can help you learn more about a great person.

Get the Facts

Use this book, and research in the library and on the internet, to find out more about your favorite Leaf. Learn as much about this player as you can. What position does he play? What are his statistics in important categories? Has he set any records? Also, be sure to write down key events in the person's life. What was his childhood like? What has he accomplished off the field? Is there anything else that makes this person special or unusual?

Use the Concept Web

A concept web is a useful research tool. Read the questions in the concept web on the following page. Answer the questions in your notebook. Your answers will help you write a biography.

Concept Web

Your Opinion
- What did you learn from the books you read in your research?
- Would you suggest these books to others?
- Was anything missing from these books?

Adulthood
- Where does this individual currently reside?
- Does he or she have a family?

Childhood
- Where and when was this person born?
- Describe his or her parents, siblings, and friends.
- Did this person grow up in unusual circumstances?

Accomplishments off the Field
- What is this person's life's work?
- Has he or she received awards or recognition for accomplishments?
- How have this person's accomplishments served others?

Write a Biography

Help and Obstacles
- Did this individual have a positive attitude?
- Did he or she receive help from others?
- Did this person have a mentor?
- Did this person face any hardships?
- If so, how were the hardships overcome?

Accomplishments on the Field
- What records does this person hold?
- What key games and plays have defined his career?
- What are his stats in categories important to his position?

Work and Preparation
- What was this person's education?
- What was his or her work experience?
- How does this person work?
- What is the process he or she uses?

Trivia Time

Take this quiz to test your knowledge of the Maple Leafs. The answers are printed upside down under each question.

1 What is the nickname for the Maple Leafs fan base?

A. Leafs Nation

2 In which two decades were the Maple Leafs most successful?

A. 1940s and 1960s

3 When did the Leafs win their most recent Stanley Cup championship?

A. 1967

4 How many Stanley Cup titles have the Maple Leafs won?

A. 13

5 What is the name of the Maple Leafs' home arena?

A. Air Canada Centre

6 Who is the interim head coach for the Leafs?

A. Peter Horachek

7 In which division do the Leafs play?

A. Atlantic

8 Before becoming the Maple Leafs, what were the two team names for Toronto's franchise?

A. The Arenas and the St. Pats

9 What are the Maple Leafs' team colors?

A. Blue and white

Key Words

All-Star: a game made for the best-ranked players in the NHL that happens mid-season. A player can be named an All-Star and then be sent to play in this game.

assists: a statistic that is attributed to up to two players of the scoring team who shoot, pass, or deflect the puck toward the scoring teammate

expanded: expansion in the NHL is marked by the addition of a new franchise. The league last expanded in 2000 when the Columbus Blue Jackets and Minnesota Wild joined the NHL.

franchise: a team that is a member of a professional sports league

hat tricks: when a player scores three goals in one game

logo: a symbol that stands for a team or organization

mascot: a character, usually an animal, that is chosen to represent a team

Original Six: the first six hockey teams that made up the NHL before the league expanded in 1967

playoffs: a series of games that occur after regular season play

rookie: a player age 26 or younger who has played no more than 25 games in a previous season, nor six or more games in two previous seasons

slap shot: a hard shot made by raising the stick about waist high before striking the puck with a sharp slapping motion

Index

Log on to www.av2books.com

AV² by Weigl brings you media enhanced books that support active learning. Go to www.av2books.com, and enter the special code found on page 2 of this book. You will gain access to enriched and enhanced content that supplements and complements this book. Content includes video, audio, weblinks, quizzes, a slide show, and activities.

AV² Online Navigation

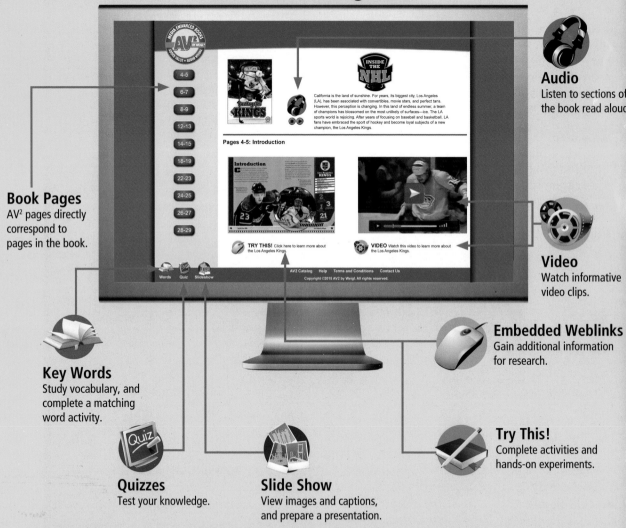

Audio
Listen to sections of the book read aloud.

Book Pages
AV² pages directly correspond to pages in the book.

Video
Watch informative video clips.

Embedded Weblinks
Gain additional information for research.

Key Words
Study vocabulary, and complete a matching word activity.

Try This!
Complete activities and hands-on experiments.

Quizzes
Test your knowledge.

Slide Show
View images and captions, and prepare a presentation.

AV² was built to bridge the gap between print and digital. We encourage you to tell us what you like and what you want to see in the future.

Sign up to be an AV² Ambassador at www.av2books.com/ambassador.

Due to the dynamic nature of the Internet, some of the URLs and activities provided as part of AV² by Weigl may have changed or ceased to exist. AV² by Weigl accepts no responsibility for any such changes. All media enhanced books are regularly monitored to update addresses and sites in a timely manner. Contact AV² by Weigl at 1-866-649-3445 or av2books@weigl.com with any questions, comments, or feedback.